This is the actual size
of the footprint of an adult wolf.

Wolves

by BETTY POLISAR REIGOT

Illustrated by FRAN STILES

SCHOLASTIC BOOK SERVICES

NEW YORK · TORONTO · LONDON · AUCKLAND · SYDNEY · TOKYO

For Tommy

Thanks to R. G. Tozer, Interpretive Services
Supervisor, Algonquin Provincial Park, Ontario,
Canada, for useful information on wolves in
the area and for permitting Deborah Arnett,
Park Naturalist, to take me on a late-night howl.
Because of Deborah's patience and persistence,
one of the Algonquin packs finally answered us.
The next day she led me to wolf tracks, the
closest we were able to come to the animals.

And I am most grateful to the late Jack Reigot
who suggested the subject of this book.

ISBN 0-590-31292-8

Text copyright © 1980 by Betty Polisar Reigot. Illustrations copyright © 1980 by
Scholastic Magazines, Inc. All rights reserved. Published by Scholastic Book Services, a
Division of Scholastic Magazines, Inc.

12 11 10 9 8 7 6 5 4 3 2 1   11   0 1 2 3 4 5/8
Printed in the U.S.A.   18

Contents

The German shepherd dog looks a lot
like a wolf, but it is not as big.

Wolves are ancestors of today's dogs and have lived on Earth for thousands of years. But scientists began to study wolves only about 40 years ago.

They went to zoos. They raised wolf puppies in their homes. They camped in the wilderness to watch wolves with binoculars.

Today, scientists use planes. From above, they can see where these beautiful, wild creatures go and what they do.

This book tells you some of the things we now know about wolves. You may be surprised to find out what wolves are really like.

The pack

Most wolves belong to a pack — a group of wolves that travel, hunt, eat, rest, play, and just hang out together much of the time. The pack is a wolf's family.

No one knows for certain, but packs probably form this way: A male and female wolf choose each other as mates. They usually stay together for at least several years.

If they have babies, the pups become part of the pack. There are from four to seven wolf pups in most litters.

Some years there is not enough food, and a few pups may starve to death. Others get sick and die. Usually, less than half the pups live long enough to become yearlings — pups that reach their first birthday.

But there is usually a new litter the next spring.

Often, other adult wolves besides the parents belong to the pack, too. There may be an aunt, an uncle, a cousin, or even a grandparent in the pack.

Once in a while, the pack lets a wolf that is not part of the family join them. We do not know why wolves sometimes let one stranger into their pack and not another.

Some packs have 20 to 30 wolves. But usually there are no more than seven members in a pack. And many packs have only two or three or four members. (We do not count newborn pups because many do not live long.)

The whole pack is one family. There are no secrets. Everybody minds everybody else's business!

Wolves — adults and pups — like to
snuggle and nuzzle and lick one another.
They rub against one another, wag their tails,
and fool around. A favorite game is tag.

How wolves get along together

When they are not hunting, most wolves are
gentle creatures. But they are not all alike.
Some are full of fun. Some are quiet. Some like
to tease and play jokes — like jumping out at
another wolf from a hiding place. Some are seri-
ous. And some get angry fast.

How do wolves feel about other wolves in the
pack? They may not care about some. They may
like others very much.

Wolves sometimes fight with each other. But most fights never go so far that wolves really hurt one another. Before that happens, one of the wolves will show that it gives up.

Maybe it will roll on its back like a puppy. Or maybe it will put its tail between its legs. The other wolf understands and stops fighting.

Animals that live in groups must understand one another. Wolves have many ways to tell other wolves what they want them to know.

A howl, a bark, a growl, a snarl, a whine, or a whimper can have a special meaning.

Wolves howl when they are happy. Sometimes they howl to find out where another pack of wolves is.

A wolf points its head to the sky when it howls. The howl sounds like a long, lonely wail that fades away at the end. But that doesn't mean the wolf is lonely or sad. A wolf may be feeling just fine when it howls.

A wolf in the forest howls. It has wandered away from its pack. It is saying, "Pack, where are you?" Usually, the pack answers with a group howl that means, "We're over here!"

A snarl or a growl often means a wolf is angry or annoyed. A bark may be a greeting, or it may be a warning.

A whine or a whimper may mean the wolf is begging for food or attention. A wolf whose mate is caught in a trap may stand nearby and whimper for hours. This may be a wolf's way of crying.

Another way wolves send messages is by marking their trails with urine. A wolf picks a spot easy for other wolves to find. The urine has a strong smell. Wolves also leave droppings — called scats — that have a strong odor, too.

The message is for other wolf packs. It says, "This is our territory. Keep out!"

But the same message can also help a stray wolf find its own pack again.

A lot of the time wolves "talk" with their bodies, especially with their heads and tails.

Wolf Dictionary

Here are some messages a wolf sends with its head:

This is the way a wolf looks when everything is okay.

This wolf is angry. It threatens to fight.

This wolf is telling another wolf — or maybe several wolves — it does not want to fight. It wants to be treated kindly.

This wolf is not sure whether it will have to fight.

A wolf that stares at another wolf is saying, "I'm the boss around here." A wolf that looks away from a stare says, "I know you're the boss around here."

Here are some messages a wolf sends with its tail:

This means the wolf is relaxed. Nothing special is going on.

 This means, "I'm a very important wolf who must be obeyed."

This means, "You are bothering me."

 This means, "You are much more important than I am. Whatever you say is all right with me!"

This means, "Don't push me around too much or I may have to fight you."

A wolf can say other things with its tail by moving it in a special way:

— A tail that sweeps back and forth means the wolf feels friendly, or playful, or happy.

— Quick, short wags of the tail, or tip of the tail, may mean the wolf doesn't feel like playing around anymore.

— A trembling tail, straight up in the air, means an important wolf is meeting another important wolf. Maybe they will be friends. Or maybe they will have to fight to decide which one is more important.

— When one wolf swings its tail against another wolf, they are having a play fight.

You can see that wolves have a rather big vocabulary.

The alpha wolf — boss of the pack

Every pack has a leader. Usually, it is the largest, strongest male. Scientists call him the alpha (**al**-fuh) wolf, which means "the first."

Most of the time, it is the alpha wolf that decides such things as:
— when the pack will travel
— which way it will go
— when to chase an animal
— where to rest
— whether to let a stranger join the pack.

Many times a day the wolves crowd around the alpha wolf. They lick his lips, nuzzle his neck, and move gently against him. In wolf language this means, "You're the boss."

After the leader, there is the second most important wolf. This may be the leader's mate, or

his friend, or another strong wolf. Then comes the next wolf . . . and so on.

Each wolf has a place in the pack. It knows which wolves must obey it — and which ones it must obey. The least important wolf is the one all the others pick on.

One day, a young male adult may feel strong enough to threaten the leader. If he becomes the leader, there may be other changes in the pack too.

The alpha wolf is usually the first to eat after a kill. When he has finished some of the best pieces of meat, he lets the other wolves eat too.

A wolf that had a certain place in the pack may try for a better place now. Maybe the new alpha wolf likes this wolf. That is enough for it to have a more important place.

Or maybe a wolf fights another pack member to decide which of the two of them is stronger. The winner and loser may then change places in the pack.

It takes a while for things to settle after a new leader takes over.

At certain times, the alpha male cannot boss everyone. He knows he must leave the alpha female alone when she cares for her babies.

Once in a while, members of the pack refuse to follow the leader. He may want to cross an icy, slippery lake. They may feel safer on a trail in the woods. So they do not move. The alpha wolf gives in to their wishes and leads them the way they want to go.

But most of the time, the alpha wolf makes sure the others know he is the leader. He is not a bully. Usually, he just has to stare at another wolf, or bare his teeth. That's enough to remind them who is in charge.

Family life

Wolf pups

Wolves usually mate in winter — between January and early March. The babies will be born about two months later. Several weeks before a mother wolf gives birth, she looks for a den.

The same den may be used year after year.

Sometimes, the den is the hollow of a large tree.

Sometimes, wolves take over the den left by a fox, or some other small animal. They must make it bigger for themselves.

Sometimes, wolves dig a deep hole in sandy ground. It is hard work. Afterwards, there is always a big pile of sand near the opening.

Many dens have tunnels and a room or two. The rooms are called chambers. The tunnels usually go about two to four meters* into the earth. But some are as long as a bus — about 10 meters**.

*about six to 13 feet
**more than 30 feet

The den is often near a hill or slope. Some of the adults rest on the high ground where they can look out for intruders and guard the den.

Some tunnels are wide enough for two wolves to pass each other. The father wolf and other adults come and go. They bring food for the mother wolf.

The mother wolf may have a chamber of her own. She needs rest before giving birth — and later on too. She may have as many as seven pups. She must feed the babies and lick each one clean. She gets tired.

At the end of a tunnel, far from the entrance, is the pups' chamber. It is the safest place in the den. It is usually made a little higher than the rest of the den so water drains down and out. That helps keep the pups dry and comfortable.

When baby wolves are born, they have dark fur, round heads, small ears, and pug noses. They weigh about ½ kilogram* and are about the size of a young kitten. The newborn pups are blind and deaf. But in a couple of weeks they will see and hear.

For the first three weeks after birth, pups stay in the den. Then they begin to play around outside.

Pups grow fast. In only two months, they weigh almost seven kilograms**.

Now that the pups are bigger and stronger, the whole pack leaves the den. They move to an open, sandy place with trees and shrubs around.

*one pound
**about 15 pounds

People who study wolves call this a rendezvous (**ron**-day-voo) site. Rendezvous means "a place to meet."

A rendezvous site may be near a brook, a stream, a river, or lake. Wolves need lots of fresh water.

The pack usually moves from one rendezvous site to another during the summer. When the pups are young, the pack may stay at a site for about three weeks. As the pups get stronger, the pack may move to a new site more often. Sometimes they spend only about a week at a rendezvous site.

Every new site is a fresh hunting ground. Moving from one site to another gets pups used to travel. By the time winter comes, they must be able to keep up with the others.

The grown-ups leave the site to hunt. While they are gone, one of the adults — not always a parent — may baby-sit. The pups need to be protected from bears and wolverines that some-times raid a site, looking for food.

By the time the pups are about seven weeks old, they need something more than their mother's milk for food. When the adult wolves hunt for themselves, they hunt for the little ones too. The adults bring meat for the pups. They carry it back in a secret, safe container — their stomachs.

The hungry pups rush over and crowd around the grown-ups when they return. They lick, nip, and kiss the adults' mouths.

This begging makes the adult bring up the food from its stomach in small amounts. The pups then eat this mushy, partly digested food a little at a time. They enjoy it!

Everyone in the pack helps care for the young. Pups crawl all over the adults — not just their parents. No one minds. Everyone is used to it.

Adults keep pups from fighting too much. They teach them their wolf "language." They show them how to hunt, when to howl, and how to take care of themselves.

A two-month-old wolf pup has a big head and big feet.

Protecting one mother and her litter is plenty of work for the pack. Everything is done to give the pups the best chance to survive.

Some years there is barely enough food for the adults. In those years, wolves do not have pups.

Growing up

Pups grow quickly. Like their dog cousins, wolf puppies run, jump, chase, climb, explore, and chew anything. They enjoy a game of tug-of-war. They learn to hunt by pouncing on mice and other small creatures.

Pups have play fights. Play fighting is important. It prepares them to take their place in the pack. One day, in a play fight, one of the pups gives up. Now those two know which one is stronger. They will not have to fight again.

All the pups are together all the time. Soon they become unfriendly to outsiders. They begin to have strong feelings of belonging to their pack — living and "working" together.

By the time a pup has become a yearling, it looks like an adult. But it is young and usually needs to be close to its parents for at least another year. It still has a lot to learn about living in the wild.

A male wolf, about two or three years old, gets restless. So he may leave the pack and look for a mate. If he finds one, the pair may start a pack of their own.

Lone wolves

A lone wolf is usually a young, healthy animal that leaves the pack to find a mate and start its own pack.

But there are lone wolves that don't belong to any pack. They may have been forced out of a pack because they are not good hunters anymore.

Or they are too old or too weak to keep up with the rest. Or maybe the other wolves in the pack just don't like them.

These wolves often follow a pack from a distance. If they come too close, the pack attacks them. Lone wolves wait to see if there is something left to eat after the pack has finished a meal.

They have a hard time. Many die.

Hunting

Wolves have no special hunting ground. They need lots of meat. So they go where there is food. Wolves don't waste energy catching small animals if large ones are around.

There are two main kinds of wolves — the *tundra wolf* and the *timber wolf.*

The tundra wolf lives far north on the treeless plains called the *tundra.*

The timber wolf lives farther south where it roams the forests and woodlands, meadows and mountains.

Deer, moose, elk, beaver, sheep, and buffalo — called bison in Europe — are the kinds of animals timber wolves like to catch when they can.

Tundra wolves that live far north —·in Alaska, in northern Canada, and in the arctic — depend mainly on large herds of caribou for food.

There may be as many as a thousand
or more caribou in a herd.

Spring and summer

In the spring and summer, the adult wolves usually set off to hunt in the early evening — often going as far as 32 kilometers* away. They return to the pups sometime during the night or the next morning.

Many animals are born in the spring, and wolves catch as many of the young of other species as they can.

Timber wolves fill in their diet with many different kinds of food. They zig-zag around looking for mice, mink, muskrat, squirrels, and rabbits. Other snacks are birds, snakes, fish, ducks, lizards, grasshoppers, and earthworms. Timber wolves also eat berries and other fruits.

Farther north, tundra wolves that must stay near newborn pups may have a hard time finding food.

During spring and summer, tundra wolves usually kill a few of the caribou that cannot keep up with the migrating herd. The wolves may cover small chunks of the meat with loose soil. This hides the meat from ravens, crows, and vultures — and keeps flies away too.

From time to time, the adults go back to these hidden animals. They eat some of the

*about 20 miles

meat and bring some back to the pups. There are not many other things to eat on the tundra — only mice, ground squirrels, arctic hares, fish, and small birds.

When winter comes

Some pack members may go off on their own in the summertime. They may be away from the pack for a few hours, a few days, or for weeks.

By the time winter comes, all the wolves in the pack gather together. It is time to set off on their winter travels. The pups will go along too. That is why packs seem larger in winter than summer.

The pack stops often, at first, to give the young ones a chance to rest. But from now until next spring they no longer return to a den or a rendezvous site.

Once in a while, two wolf families join to make an extra large pack. But they split up to hunt. If too many wolves go after the same animal, they may get in each other's way.

Many people think wolves see an animal and decide, "Mmm, there's a nice dinner!" and then

Wolves follow the leader. Going one behind the other is easier than making new tracks in deep snow.

just attack and tear the creature apart. That is not what happens most of the time.

Wolves must travel to find, catch, and kill what they eat.

When they travel, wolves jog at a steady pace — about eight kilometers* an hour. They can go for about nine hours without stopping.

Wolves choose places that are easy for them to run along. A wolf trail may be a narrow path in one place,

    — then a wide valley,
    — go up and over a mountain,
    — be part of a railroad track,
    — or part of a human hunter's path,
    — and even include part of a highway.

*five miles

Short trails criss-cross inside larger trails. A pack may go back to some part of a trail at any time — in a few hours, in a few days, or a few weeks later. The trails of different packs may overlap for a short distance.

Wolves use some trails over and over. Young wolves learn the trails from their parents. Many trails may have been used for hundreds of years.

How wolves catch their prey

Most of the time, wolves find prey by smell.
Wind — even a light breeze — carries the scent
of an animal to wolves before they see it.

As soon as they get a whiff, wolves gather
close to the leader. They point their noses in the
direction of the smell. Then, single file, they follow the leader to the smell.

A pack of wolves in an open area forms a circle, nose to nose, like football players in a huddle. Wolves wag their tails for a moment before starting the hunt.

They are careful to move against the wind. (If the wind comes from behind the wolves and blows toward the prey, the prey will smell wolves and probably run away.)

Once in a while, wolves will follow tracks made by an animal until they find the animal that made them.

Sometimes, wolves find prey just by luck. They may happen to surprise a deer, or some other animal.

Each kind of prey has a way to escape or to protect itself.

Caribou, deer, and elk run fast. They jump easily over logs, stumps, and rocks. Wolves may have a hard time catching up with them.

Mountain sheep climb rocky cliffs. Wolves that travel along high mountain paths may try to drive the sheep down and make them stumble and fall.

One of the largest prey that timber wolves hunt is moose. A healthy moose that does not run can fight off a pack of wolves. It rears up, twists around quickly, strikes out with hind and front feet. A kick from one of its powerful hooves can kill a wolf.

If the moose runs, one wolf usually grabs it by the nose and hangs on. Then the others lunge at the moose from all sides.

Hunting is hard work. Many times wolves chase an animal and never catch it. Often, they must go without food for days.

The animals wolves catch are usually ones that cannot keep up with the rest of their group. They are mainly prey that are old, very young, or weak. Or they may be sick or injured.

A moose that is attacked by wolves and stays to fight will back against a nearby tree or rock, if it can, for more protection.

Making a kill

As they get near their prey, wolves wag their tails. They hold their heads low and look sharply ahead. They try to get very close without being seen. This is called stalking.

When the prey sees the wolves, it may not move. The wolves stop. They keep watching it. Sometimes they move forward very slowly.

If the animal runs, wolves will rush it. Like

other dogs, wolves like to run after something that moves.

They take great leaps to reach the animal quickly. They try to hurt or wound the creature. If the prey loses blood, it gets weak and slows down. If it tears a muscle, or breaks a bone, it cannot run fast. It may not be able to run at all.

When they make a kill, wolves devour great chunks of meat at a time. A wolf can eat as much as nine kilograms* at one feeding. That amount of meat would be enough for 40 people.

If a small pack kills a big prey animal, wolves eat as much as they can and then find a place to rest. A few hours later — often, at night — they return to finish and gnaw the bones.

After a big meal, wolves need lots of water. They lap it up with their tongues.

Then they travel to an open space, or the edge of a mountain. They stretch out on their sides or bellies in the sun. In bad weather, wolves curl up under evergreen trees or in any other protected spot. They enjoy a rest while they digest their food.

After a while, they get restless. Before they start to travel again, wolves may gather around the alpha wolf. They wag their tails. Then, one by one, they begin to howl until they are all singing together.

*about 20 pounds

Will there always be wolves?

Troubles began for wolves when humans learned how to farm. People needed land. They cut back the wilderness to grow food and raise animals.

Wild creatures had to find other places to live. Some of these animals were the usual prey for wolves. When they left, wolves had to find other food. It was easy for wolves to catch cattle, horses, goats, sheep, and other domestic animals.

This made farmers and ranchers angry. And people who hunted for sport did not want wolves around because wolves and people hunt the same wild animals.

People tried every way to get rid of wolves. They used traps, poison, guns, and other deadly weapons. A reward was given to anyone who killed a wolf. The reward was called a bounty.

Today, people are beginning to understand that all creatures have a place on Earth. We have learned a good deal about wolves. We know that wolves kill because they must eat.

Most of the time, wolves kill sick, weak, and old animals. And sometimes they go after very young animals when there are a lot of them. This helps keep healthy, strong animals of a species alive.

Wolves also provide food for other animals. Whatever wolves leave after a kill feeds ravens, crows, jay birds, eagles, foxes, weasels, and other small creatures.

There used to be wolves in most of North America, the British Isles, Europe, the Middle East, India, Russia, China, and Japan.

Today, most wolves that we know about are in Alaska, Canada, the northern United States, some countries of Europe, eastern Europe, and Asia. There are a few wolves in Mexico.

The wolves that most scientists have been studying are in Canada and the northern United States.

Scientists believe healthy wolves do not prey on humans. They say there is no proof that a wolf ever attacked a person in North America. Wolves that come near people are usually just curious. Then they go away. Most of the time they are too shy even to come close.

But a few experts — and some Eskimos that live closer to wolves than most other humans — believe wolves do attack people. There is still a lot we do not know about wolves.

In the Soviet Union, bounties are given to encourage people to kill wolves. Today bounties are not often given in North America. But many wolves up north are killed anyway.

We must protect farmers, ranchers, and even hunters. But we must protect wolves too.

Wild creatures have lived in the wilderness for millions of years. We can save part of our wilderness for them. Forest rangers can help keep the few areas left in good condition. Laws can provide special places where wolves can live free and unharmed.

If we do not do this now, soon there will be no wolves. We will lose one of Earth's most beautiful, intelligent, and interesting animals.